All About the Seasons
ACTIVITY BOOK

by Tara Doyle

Illustrated by Patricia Hammel

SCHOLASTIC INC.
New York   Toronto   London   Auckland   Sydney

No part of this publication may be reproduced in whole or in part, or stored in a retrieval system, or transmitted in any form or by any means, electronic, mechanical, photocopying, recording, or otherwise, without written permission of the publisher. For information regarding permission write to Scholastic Inc., 730 Broadway, New York, NY 10003.

ISBN 0-590-46296-2

Copyright © 1992 by Scholastic Inc.
All rights reserved. Published by Scholastic Inc.

16 15 14 13   5 6 7/9

.S.A.   34

First Scholastic printing, September 1992

You can check your answers to the puzzles on pages 31 and 32.

Matching Seasons

One year is made up of four seasons: winter, spring, summer, and fall.
There are twelve months in a year and each season lasts about three months.

Draw a line from the name of the season to the picture of that season.

1

2

WINTER, SPRING, SUMMER, FALL

3

4

Winter Fun

In the winter the earth is tilted away from the sun. So the weather gets very, very cold.
But there are lots of fun things to do outside if you bundle up!
Circle the people on the hill who are <u>not</u> doing winter activities.

One-of-a-Kind Snowflakes

Clouds are made up of teeny tiny drops of water.
When the temperature falls below freezing,
the drops become ice crystals.
The crystals clump together and form big,
fluffy snowflakes.
And no two snowflakes are alike!

Look at the numbered snowflakes in this box. One is missing from each row. Write the number of the missing snowflake in the space provided.

Snowbound!

A *nimbostratus* cloud is a low, dark, gray cloud. In the summer it brings rain. But in the cold, cold winter it brings snow.

A big snowstorm is coming! Help the boy sled to safety through the maze.

Frosty the Snowman

Hooray for snow! You can build a snow fort, have a snowball fight, or you can make a giant snowman!

Complete these two frosty snowpeople.

The Shadow Knows

Every February 2nd is Groundhog Day. If the groundhog sees his shadow today, it means that there are still six more weeks of winter. But if he doesn't see his shadow, it means there might be an early spring. Yaay!

Connect the dots to see what a groundhog looks like.

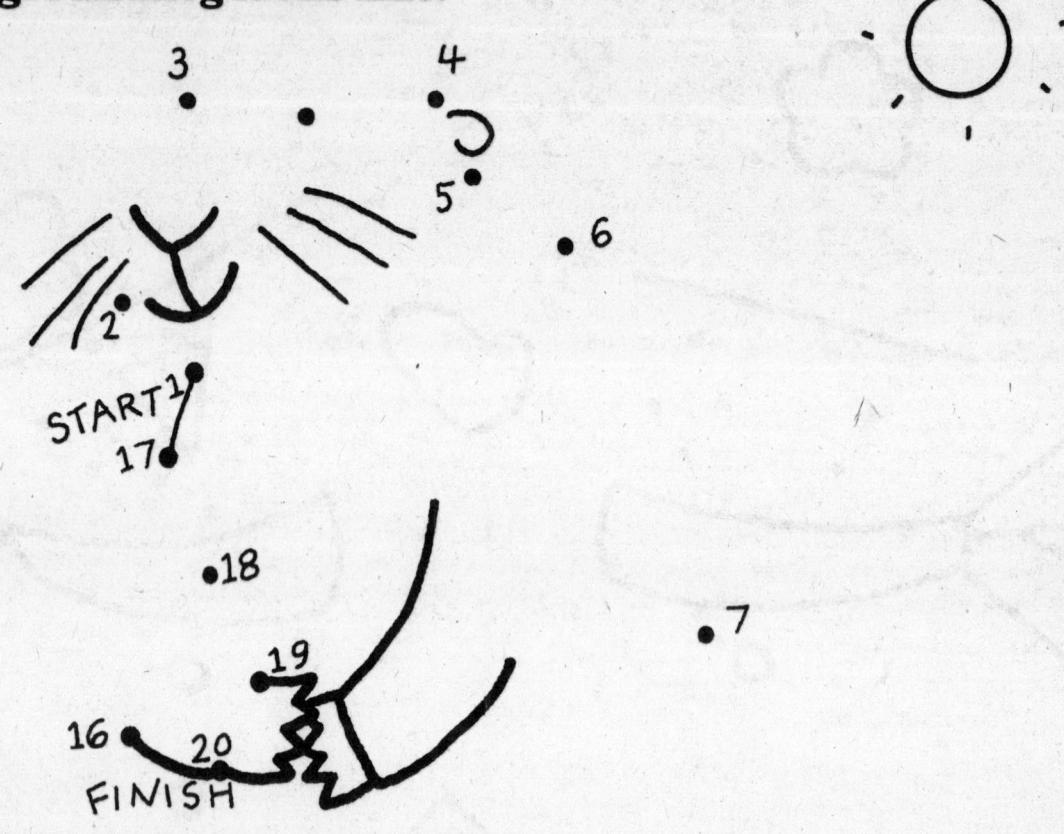

What's Missing?

Brrr! When it's cold we wear a coat, mittens, scarf, and a hat to keep warm.
**The two pictures below are *almost* the same.
In the second picture there are seven things missing.
Circle the places where the missing things should be.**

Spring Has Sprung!
What comes after winter? Spring!
In spring, the days start to get longer and warmer.
Animals come out of hibernation.
And trees and flowers get buds and bloom.
Color this spring scene using this color key.
Color the spaces numbered 1 GREEN.
Color the spaces numbered 2 PINK.
Color the spaces numbered 3 YELLOW.
Color the spaces numbered 4 RED.
Color the spaces numbered 5 BROWN.

Smell the Flowers!
**The names of these spring flowers are hidden in the word search:
CROCUS, DAISY, TULIP, DAFFODIL, MARIGOLD, LILAC.
Find and circle them. The words go up, down, diagonally, and sideways.**

```
B D S H U E S O R
M A R I G O L D G
J F V L P Y Z A E
S F T C M T P I O
C O K Q R A B S H
Z D S W U O N Y X
P I L U T E C F N
M L I L A C W U K
Y A D S X D R G S
```

April Showers Bring May Flowers

Millions of tiny droplets of water inside clouds join together to make bigger drops. When the drops get too big and heavy, they fall to the ground... *plop* ... *plop* ... and become raindrops!

Circle the things you would need on a rainy spring day.

Tweet! Tweet!

Unscramble the names of these spring birds: ROBIN, SPARROW, BLUEJAY, FINCH, CARDINAL. Each letter in a name is numbered. Starting with number 1, place the letter that goes with 1 in the first box, the letter that goes with 2 in the second box, and keep going until each box is filled. One is already done for you.

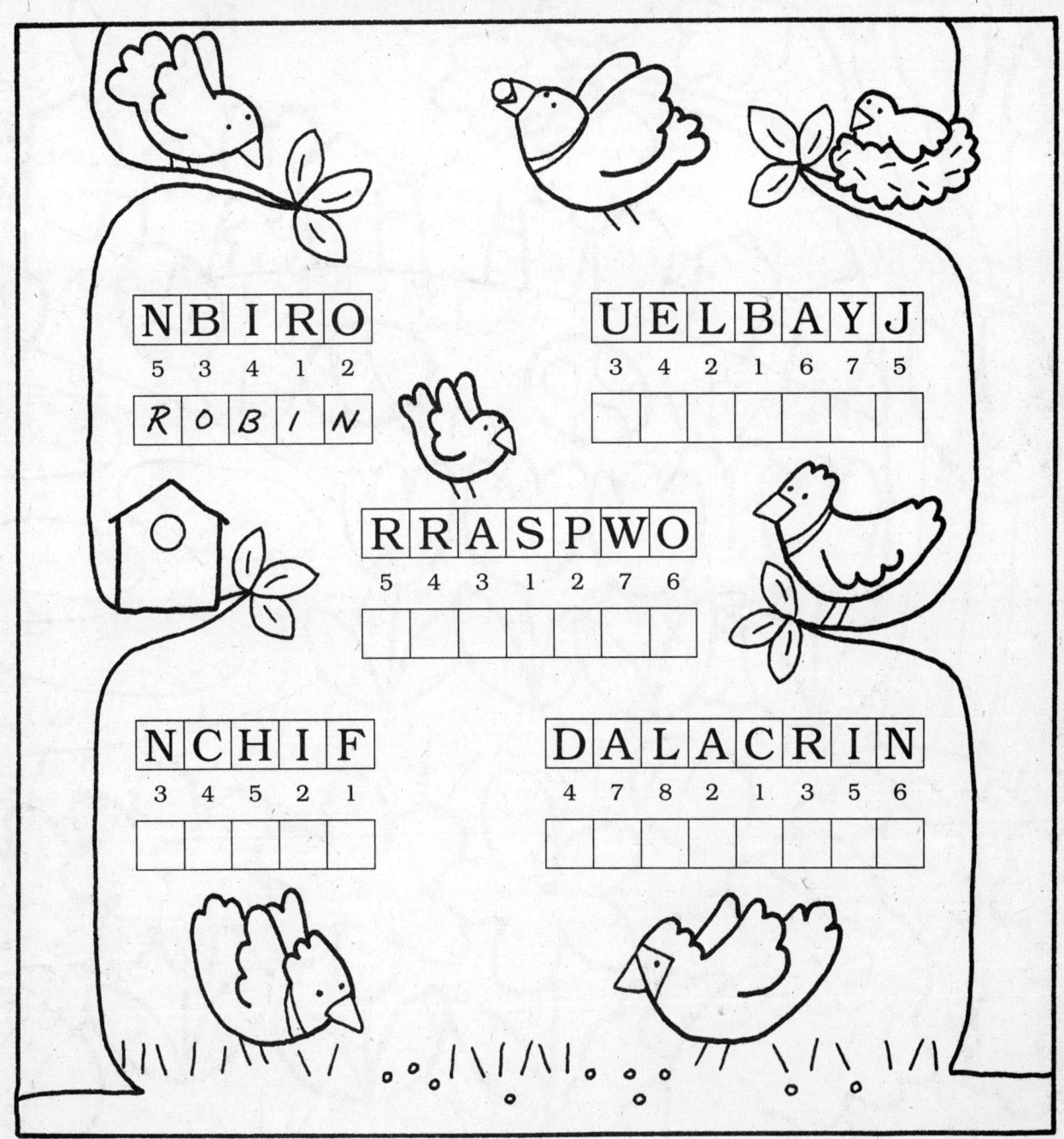

A Bunny Hunt!

Spring brings a special holiday called Easter. The Easter bunny brings baskets of colored eggs and yummy chocolate.

Find the 10 hidden bunny rabbits in this picture and circle them.

Sunny Days

What comes after spring? Summer!
Summer days are long and warm.
It's fun to play baseball or have a picnic outdoors!
Connect the dots to make a giant sun!

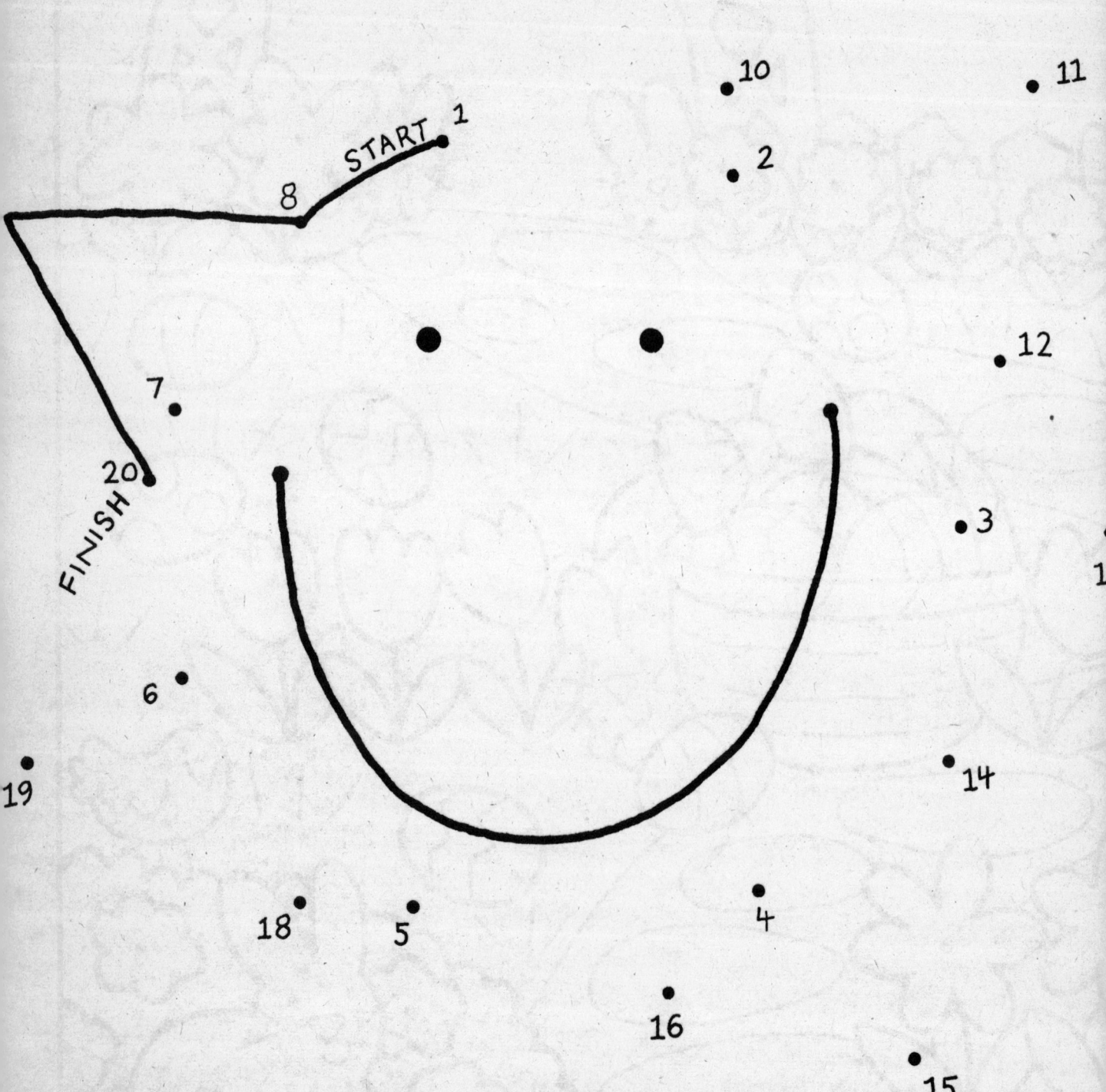

Stormy Weather

Sometimes in a rainstorm there is a giant electric bolt in the sky called lightning. Shortly after you see a lightning flash, you will hear a booming noise from the air. Yikes!

To find out the name of this noise, begin at start and go around the circle twice. Starting with the first box, write every other letter in the spaces below.

Summer Fun

It's very warm in the summer because the earth is tilted toward the sun.
In the summertime it's fun to go play at the beach. But don't forget your suntan lotion. If the sun is very hot you can get sunburn!
Follow the maze and help get the girl to the shady umbrella.

START

FINISH

18

Day at the Beach
Circle the things you might need for a day at the beach.

Red, White, and Blue

Every summer on the Fourth of July we celebrate Independence Day. On this happy holiday, many people have a big barbecue and watch fireworks light up the sky!

Color this scene and remember what you see. Then take the memory test on the next page.

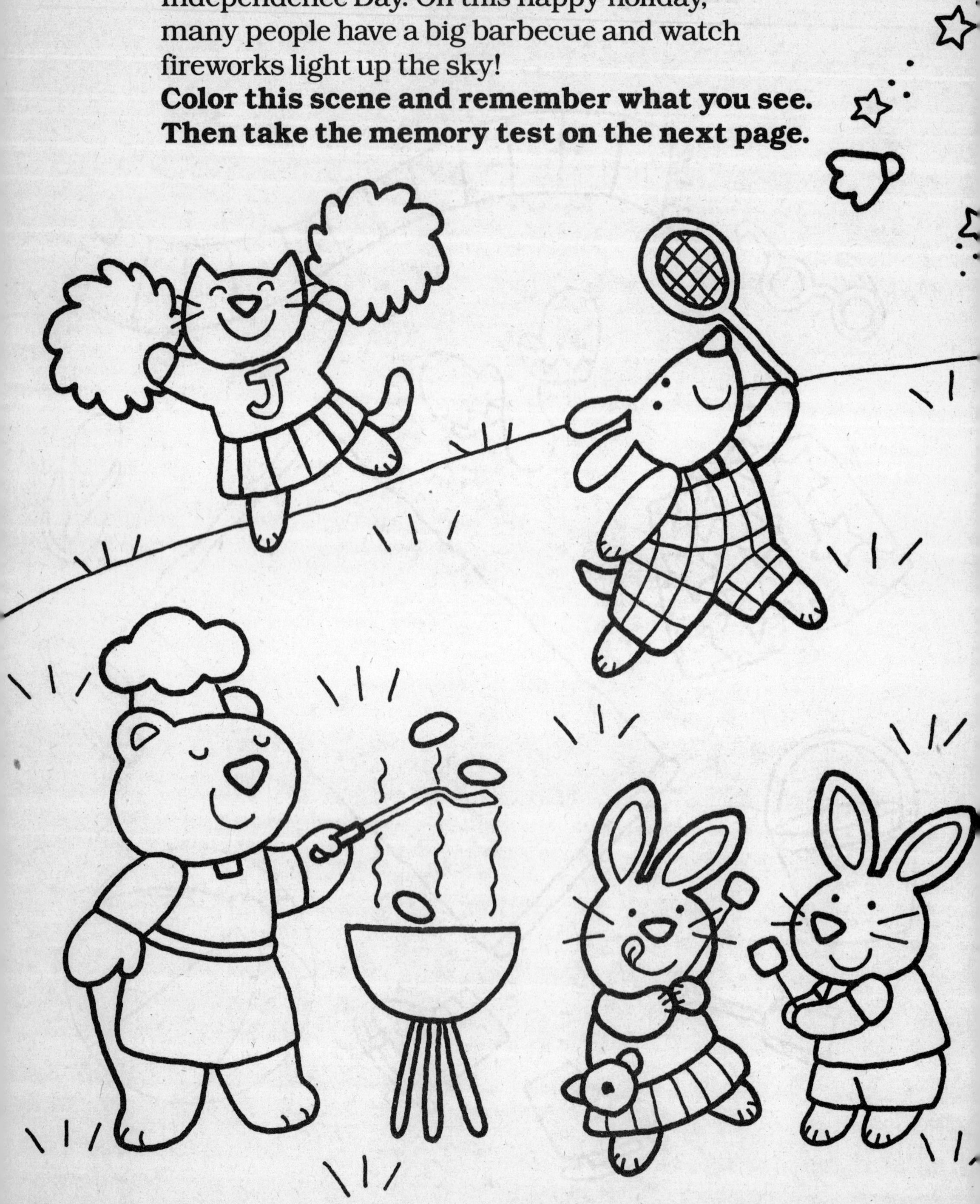

Can You Remember?
Circle the picture in each scene that is exactly the same as the one on pages 20 and 21.

Let's Fly South

When summer ends, fall (autumn) begins.
It starts to get colder, so birds fly south
to find warmer weather.
Circle the two birds that are exactly the same.

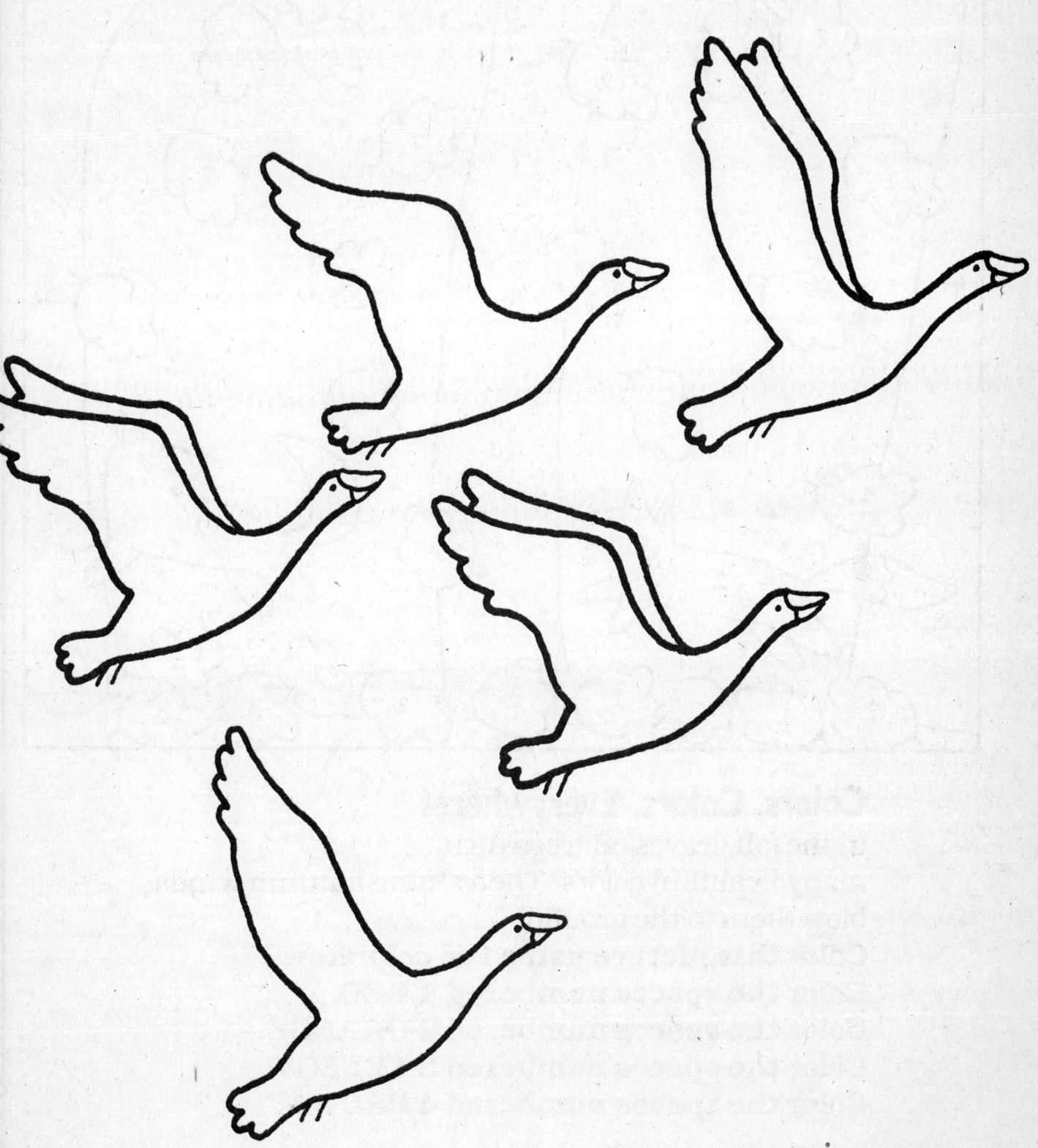

Colors, Colors, Everywhere!
In the fall, leaves on trees turn many beautiful colors. Then strong autumn winds blow them to the ground!
Color this picture using the color key.
Color the spaces numbered 1 RED.
Color the spaces numbered 2 ORANGE.
Color the spaces numbered 3 YELLOW.
Color the spaces numbered 4 BROWN.

Trick-or-Treat

The last day of October is a scary fall holiday. Everyone dresses up in costumes and goes trick-or-treating.

What is this holiday called? To find out, cross out all the boxes that do not equal 9. Then write the letters that are left in the spaces below.

W	H	G	A	L	B	L	O	Y	W	E	S	E	T	N
2+2	5+4	3+1	8+1	2+7	7+3	3+6	9+0	9+1	7+2	4+5	2+4	6+3	6+2	1+8

__ __ __ __ __ __ __ __ __

25

Apple Orchard

Apples on trees become ripe, juicy,
and ready for picking in the fall.
Apple picking is fun!
And homemade apple pie is yum, yum!
**There are three trees in this orchard.
Circle and count how many apples are on each tree
and write the number on the line below.
Which tree has the most apples?**

___   ___   ___

Nutty Squirrels

Animals get ready to hibernate by gathering enough food to last the whole winter. Squirrels spend their days collecting nuts and seeds.
**How many hidden nuts can you find?
Circle them all.**

Yummy, Yummy for the Tummy!

Thanksgiving is in November. Friends and family celebrate this holiday together with a *mmm, mmm,* good meal.

Solve the crossword to see the names of things you eat on Thanksgiving. Use the word list to help you guess what each picture is. Then write the correct word in the crossword.

Down

Word List
Squash
Pumpkin
Pies
Turkey
Corn
Cranberry

Across

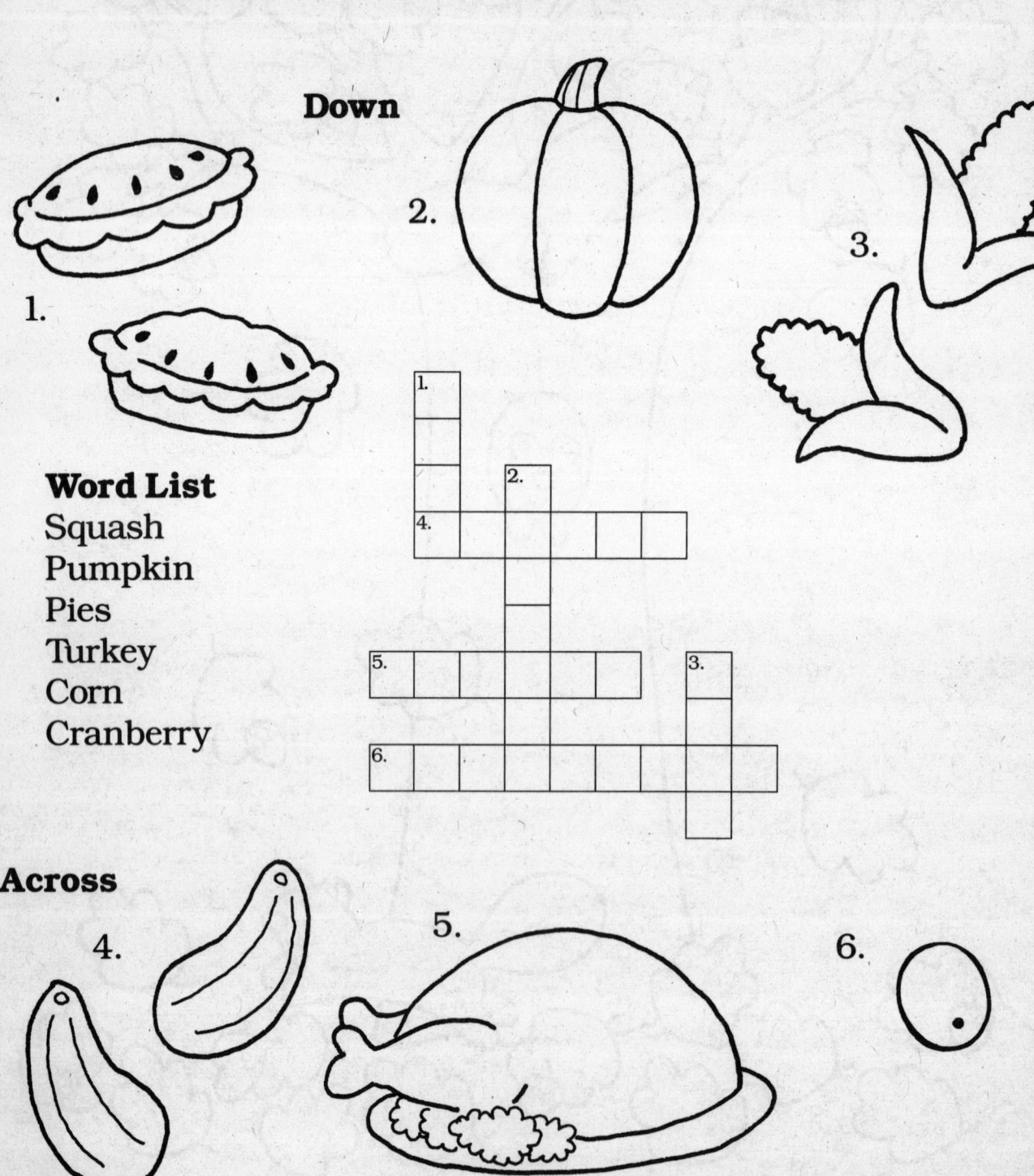

The Four Seasons

**The names of four seasons are hidden in the word search:
WINTER, SPRING, SUMMER, and FALL.
Find and circle them.
The words go up, down, diagonally, and sideways.**

```
S A B O C I M H P
P U Q K N L L A F
T R M U I D Y Z M
B S C M F E T E G
E G I L E X K N W
W I N T E R I U D
A V R J Y R V A G
F C E Z P S X P W
Q L N S R B O J H
```

Monthly Match

There are three months in every season.
Match the months that go with each season.

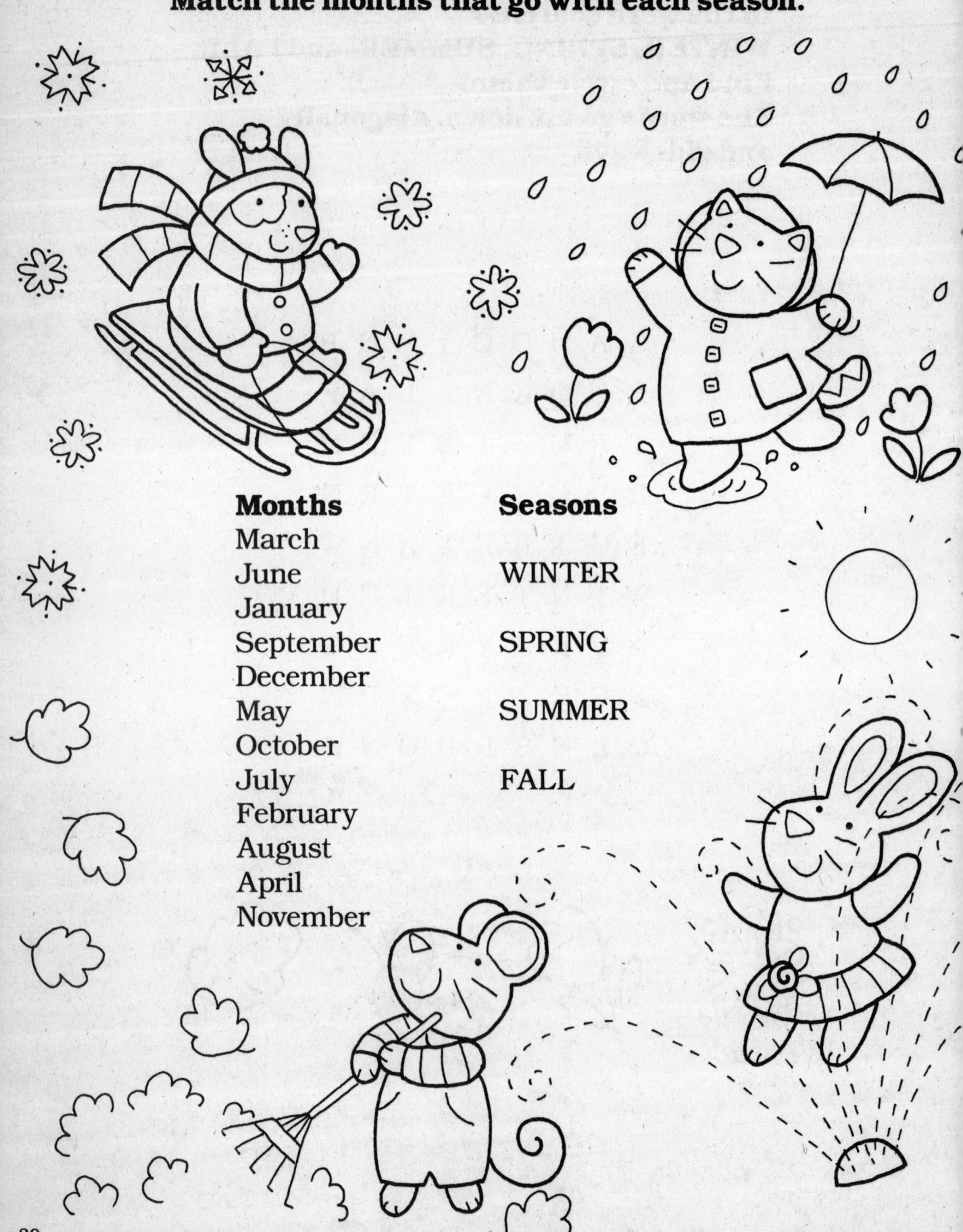

Months
March
June
January
September
December
May
October
July
February
August
April
November

Seasons

WINTER

SPRING

SUMMER

FALL

PUZZLE ANSWERS

Page 3. Matching Seasons

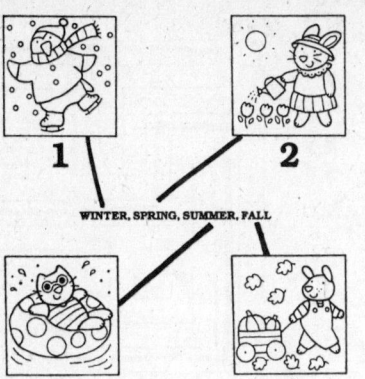

Page 4. Winter Fun

Page 5. One-of-a-Kind Snowflakes

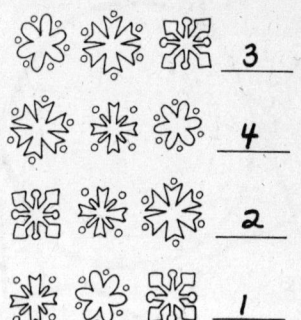

Page 6. Snowbound!

Page 7. Frosty the Snowman

Page 8. The Shadow Knows

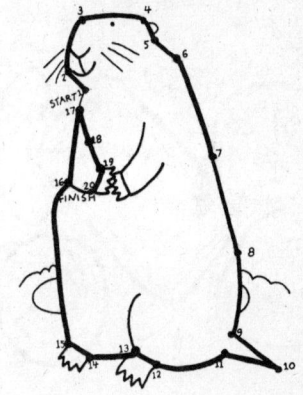

Page 9. What's Missing?

Page 11. Smell the Flowers!

Page 12. April Showers Bring May Flowers

Page 13. Tweet! Tweet!
BLUEJAY, SPARROW, FINCH, CARDINAL

Pages 14-15. A Bunny Hunt!

31

Page 16. Sunny Days

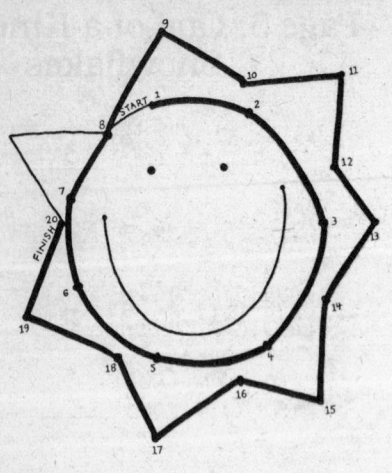

Page 17. Stormy Weather
THUNDER

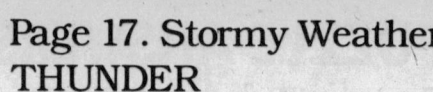

Page 18. Summer Fun

Page 19. Day at the Beach

Page 22. Can You Remember?

Page 23. Let's Fly South

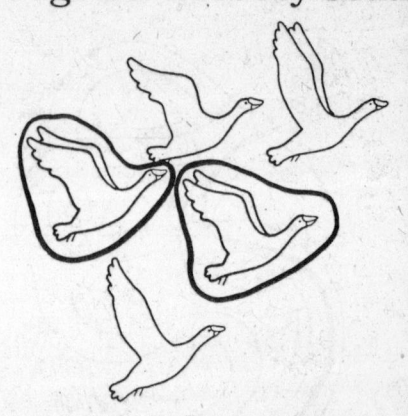

Page 25. Trick-or-Treat
HALLOWEEN

Page 26. Apple Orchard

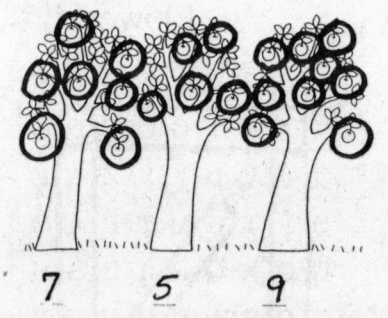

The last tree has the most apples.

Page 27. Nutty Squirrels

There are 10 nuts.

Page 28. Yummy, Yummy for the Tummy!

Page 29. The Four Seasons

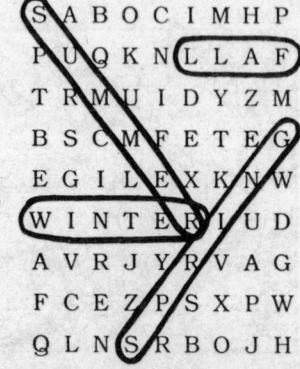

Page 30. Monthly Match

32